V is for Venus Flytrap

A Plant Alphabet

Written by Eugene Gagliano and Illustrated by Elizabeth Traynor

ILLUSTRATOR'S ACKNOWLEDGMENTS

My grateful thanks to the friends and family who helped me through the journey of this book, especially Brian Scatasti for his summer of assistance, my mother, Betsy Traynor, MD for her support, and my models and their families for their graceful posing: Ellen Dunlavey and dad Rob (A, M, V), Pierre and Victoire Draps (D, R), Georgeanne Verbeek (M), Lucy Pawliczek (P), Ellen Bragg (R), Lily Bragg (W), Sophia Thomas (W) and dad Sean (Z), plus my four-legged friends: Hogarth (F), Joralemon (L), Junebug (M), Zoe's Panda (Q), and Sammie the Vegetarian Chihuahua (V).

Lastly, a heartfelt thank you to Felicia Macheske, Amy Lennex, and Heather Hughes at Sleeping Bear Press for their patience (again!).

Sleeping Bear Press™
310 North Main Street, Suite 300
Chelsea, MI 48118
www.sleepingbearpress.com

© 2009 Sleeping Bear Press is an imprint of Gale, a part of Cengage Learning.

Printed and bound in the United States.

First Edition

10 9 8 7 6 5 4 3 2 1

Library of Congress Cataloging-in-Publication Data

Gagliano, Eugene M.
V is for venus flytrap : a plant alphabet / written by Eugene Gagliano; illustrated by Elizabeth Traynor.
p. cm.
Summary: "The plant world is explored from A to Z, with a poem to introduce each letter topic and expository text that provides letter topic details. Topics include annuals, carnivorous plants, fruit, kelp, succulent, and xeriscape"—Provided by publisher.
ISBN 978-1-58536-350-6
1. Plants—Juvenile literature. 2. Alphabet books—Juvenile literature. I. Traynor, Elizabeth. II. Title.
QK49.G32 2009
580—dc22   2008040832

This book is dedicated to Mrs. Lynch, who first sparked my interest in gardening; to Mom and Dad for letting me garden; my godfather, Carmen, for buying me my first gardening magazine; my friend Doris for giving me my first gardening book; for Mr. Thorn who encouraged my interest in gardening; for all my gardening friends; and especially for my wife, Carol, children, and grandchildren, who support my gardening passion.

GENE

To Dad, for cosmos, primroses, and the brush in my hand,
and to Mac, for crocuses, ginkgoes, and the birds in the trees.
I miss you both.

Also my profound gratitude to Sean Thomas, my painting partner for this book. Mille grazie!

ELIZABETH

A is for the Annuals
we plant each year from seed.
Petunia pots and marigolds—
sun and water's what they need.

An annual plant completes its life cycle in one growing season. It grows from a seed, produces flowers, and makes new seeds that can be planted again, and then it dies. Annuals do not tolerate frost and do not survive winter. Some common annuals are begonias, snapdragons, marigolds, zinnias, and bachelor's buttons.

Most vegetables like corn, beets, radishes, and potatoes are annuals, but some vegetables are perennial and live for many years, like asparagus, rhubarb, and the Jerusalem artichoke.

The flowers of many annual plants are often used in salads; chamomile has a sweet delicate taste; borage tastes like cucumber; and the dramatic purple or yellow pansy petals liven up any salad.

Nasturtiums were regarded as a gourmet item in the days when people were self-sufficient, or lived off the land and raised their own food. Their flower buds and seeds were pickled and served as a condiment with meat. The peppery leaves were added to salads. In the 1850s the flowers were grown for eating and not for their beauty.

Bulb begins with letter **B**,
source of springtime flowers—
tulips, crocus, daffodils,
thrive on April showers.

Tulip

Daffodil

Crocus

BULBS

Tulip

Daffodil

Crocus

The common definition of a bulb is an underground storage unit of a plant. Bulbs are usually perennials and have a period of growth and flowering followed by a period of dormancy, or rest, where they die back to the ground at the end of the growing season.

Onions are an example of a bulb plant. Slicing onion bulbs causes cells to be broken and to eventually generate sulfenic acid, which becomes a volatile gas. When the gas reaches the eye it reacts with water in the eye and produces a dilute solution of sulfuric acid. This irritates the nerve endings in the eye, making it sting, causing tears.

Other uses for bulb plants include the fall flowering crocus, used to make saffron, the world's most expensive spice. It takes more than seventy-five thousand flowers to produce a pound of saffron. Daffodils are used as a symbol of hope for the American Cancer Society.

Carnivorous animals eat other animals. Carnivorous plants attract, capture, and kill animal life forms, and then digest and absorb the nutrients from them. Carnivorous plants use five basic trapping mechanisms: pitfall traps, flypaper traps, snap traps, bladder traps, and lobster pot traps.

Many people enjoy growing the Venus flytrap, an example of a snap trap plant. The Venus flytrap has trigger hairs on its lobed leaves that cause the leaf to close and trap insects. Prodding the traps to watch them close and feeding them cheese and other inappropriate items can cause the death of the plant.

Another carnivorous plant is the pitcher plant, which derives nutrients by trapping and consuming insects. It is an example of a pitfall trap. It traps its prey in a rolled leaf that contains a pool of digestive enzymes or bacteria.

Carnivorous plants often grow in thin soils or soils poor in nutrients, especially nitrogen, like acidic bogs or rock outcroppings. Most carnivorous houseplants require rainwater or distilled water. Water from the tap or drinking water contains minerals that build up and can quickly kill the plants.

Carnivorous for letter C,
   the insect-eating kind,
plants that are unusual
   and sometimes hard to find.

Deciduous plants shed their leaves every year. Leaves get their green color from chlorophyll, a pigment that enables them to process sunlight during photosynthesis. In autumn, chlorophyll production ceases as night length increases, allowing leaves to show their yellow, orange, and red colors. Warm sunny days and cool, frostless nights seem to create the most spectacular color displays in autumn. Sugar is produced in the leaves of some trees on warm, fall days, and then trapped by the chill of night. The accumulated sugars cause the leaves to turn a brighter red.

A deciduous tree, the maple tree, produces very sweet sap. Maple syrup is made from boiling the sap, or clear liquid that circulates in the maple tree. It becomes syrup when most of the water has boiled off and the sugar content reaches 67 percent.

Only healthy maple trees, about 10 inches in diameter (which is about 40 years old) can be tapped. If cared for properly, a maple tree can produce sap for a hundred years or more. It takes about 40 gallons of sap to make one gallon of syrup.

D d

D is for Deciduous—
bushes, vines, and trees,
that change to autumn colors
and gently drop their leaves.

Sugar Maple

Ginkgo

White Oak

White Pine

Fraser Fir

Black Spruce

E e

Evergreens begin with **E**,
and some are conifers,
staying green all winter
like the pine, the spruce, and firs.

Evergreens have needlelike leaves or flat, scalelike leaves that stay green throughout the year. Conifers are evergreens that bear cones. The most common conifers are pines, spruce, cedars, fir, and redwoods. There are many evergreens that are not conifers like holly, rhododendron, and wintercreeper.

In the White Mountains of California you will find one of the oldest trees now living, a bristlecone pine called "Methuselah." According to the *Guinness Book of World Records*, the tree is estimated to be 4,733 years old. The tallest tree in North America is the redwood, some measuring more than 300 feet tall.

Each year the famous Christmas tree in Rockefeller Center is decorated with 30,000-plus lights as the official beginning of the holiday season. The tradition began in 1931 when construction workers building the center put up the first tree. In 1933 the first formal tree lighting took place. In 1948 the tallest tree ever displayed measured 100 feet tall. Trees have come from as far away as Ottawa, Ontario, in Canada.

Ff

Winesap Apple Orchard

In botany, the study of plants and how they grow, a fruit is defined as the ripened ovary and seed-bearing part of a flowering plant; an apple core, for example. Many people commonly refer to a fruit as parts of the plant that are edible, sweet, and fleshy. According to botanists, cucumbers, squash, peppers, and tomatoes are considered fruits and are called botanical fruits.

Citrus fruits, like oranges and lemons, and their juices are one of the highest sources of vitamin C. Vitamin C, also known as ascorbic acid, is a water-soluble vitamin necessary for normal growth and development. The human body cannot store vitamin C. Unlike most mammals, humans cannot make their own vitamin C and must get it through their diet. California and Florida are the nation's largest orange-producing states, and the orange blossom is the state flower of Florida.

Another healthy fruit, the cranberry, is primarily grown in five states: Oregon, Washington, Massachusetts, Wisconsin, and New Jersey. Cranberries grow on a vine that requires an ample water supply. Cranberry fields, which can be 75 to 100 years old, are flooded to harvest the berries.

Fruit begins with letter F.
There're many kinds you'll see.
Berries, apples, grapes, and pears—
good food for you and me.

Gala
Apple

Granny
Smith
Apple

Bosc Pear

Bartlett
Pear

Gg

Cereal crops or grains are mostly grasses cultivated for their edible grains or seeds. Maize, or corn, wheat, and rice account for most of the world's grain production.

The word cereal is derived from Ceres, the Roman goddess of harvest and agriculture.

Whole grains have not had the bran, or outer protective shell, removed in the milling process. Whole grain products are high in dietary fiber, a component of plant foods that moves through the digestive system, absorbing water, helping to get rid of body wastes. If an ingredient list has *whole wheat*, *whole meal*, or *whole corn* as the first ingredient, the product is a whole-grain food item. Whole grains have been shown to reduce the likelihood of some cancers, digestive system diseases, gum disease, coronary heart disease, diabetes, and obesity. Common whole grain products are oatmeal, popcorn, brown rice, and whole wheat bread.

Nebraska, Iowa, Illinois, Indiana, Minnesota, and Ohio produce nearly 70 percent of the total United States' corn crop. These Midwest states and small parts of others are known as the "corn belt." Iowa is the largest producer of corn in the U.S.

Barley

Rye

Oats

Wheat

Rice

G is for the many Grains,
wheat, barley, oats, and rye,
found in breads and cereals.
You should give them all a try.

An herb is a plant used as a medicine or as a seasoning in the kitchen. Mint is a favorite garden herb. There are many kinds of mint besides the commonly known peppermint and spearmint, such as apple mint, pineapple mint, orange mint, chocolate mint and curly mint. Mint is used to flavor beverages, sauces, salads, baked goods, and ice cream.

Parsley is rich in vitamin C and has a reputation for curing bad breath, especially that caused by lots of garlic. The roots of chicory are sometimes roasted for a healthy caffeine-free alternative to coffee. For many centuries rosemary was thought to be a cure for lethargy and dullness of mind. The common foxglove, *Digitalis purpurea*, used to treat cardiac malfunction, is poisonous in its raw state. The sap of the *Aloe vera*, or burn plant, is made into an ointment and used as an antiseptic to heal wounds and burns.

H is for the garden Herbs.
Come and take a look.
They add flavor to our meals
and help us when we cook.

Ii

I is for the Important role
of plants in the world today—
for shelter, food, and oxygen
and more I have to say.

Conservation and protection of the environment is important because humans depend on ecosystems such as forests, bogs, prairies, and wetlands for storm protection, clean water, fertile soils, food, fuel, and flood control. An ecosystem is a community of organisms together with their physical environment.

Trees filter and trap pollutants such as smoke, dust, and ash, making the air we breathe cleaner. Tree roots hold the soil together and absorb water to help reduce the effects of flooding. They also provide food, medicine, and building materials. The importance of trees is illustrated in a children's book by Dr. Seuss titled *The Lorax*.

Trees absorb massive amounts of carbon dioxide from our atmosphere and in turn give off oxygen. This is important because the Earth's temperature rises as gases in the atmosphere trap heat from the sun—the Greenhouse Effect.

Some Native Americans use aspen bark for reducing fever and fighting influenza.

Jj

A jungle is defined as land that is densely overgrown with tropical vegetation. A rainforest is a dense, broadleaf, largely evergreen forest occurring mostly in tropical regions of the world that receive large amounts of rain. The Amazon region of South America contains one of the world's largest rainforests. Half of the world's plant and animal species live in tropical rainforests.

Tropical rainforests are warm and moist, while temperate rainforests are cool. Temperate rainforests are found along coasts in the temperate zone, such as the Pacific Northwest of the United States. Both are endangered!

Both tropical and temperate rainforests are very lush and wet. Rainfall comes regularly throughout the year. Many important products originate in the rainforest such as coffee, chocolate, vanilla, and a variety of medicines.

Rainforests and jungles are part of the forest biome. Some other biomes include: freshwater, marine, desert, grassland, and tundra. A biome is a large, distinctive complex of plant communities created and maintained by climate.

J is for Jungle or rainforest—
an important place you'll see,
alive with green vegetation
and wild animals running free.

Kelp is for the letter **K**
growing in the ocean,
reaching toward the sunlight
in a swaying motion.

K
k

Aquatic plants live in water. Kelp is a kind of aquatic plant that grows in seawater. It can grow up to 35 inches a day. Kelp forests grow in clear, shallow ocean water, offering protection and food for some sea creatures. Air bladders, hollow air-filled structures attached to the seaweed, help keep the kelp blades close to the surface, so they can use the sun's energy to make food.

Kelp ash is rich in iodine and alkali and is used in soap and glass production. *Alginate*, a kelp-derived carbohydrate, is used to thicken products like ice cream, salad dressing, jelly, and toothpaste. Kelp is also used to make fertilizers.

A legume is a nitrogen-fixing plant. It takes nitrogen from the air and, using certain bacteria found in its root nodules changes it into nitrates, making it usable by the plant. Legumes help restore available nitrogen to the soil. Farmers use legumes like alfalfa, clover, and vetch in crop rotation to replenish soil that has been depleted of nitrogen.

Legumes such as peas, beans, and lentils are all sources of protein, iron, and fiber. Many traditional dairy products such as milk, yogurt, and cream cheese have been imitated using processed soybeans.

A "dry" bean is any bean pod that has ripened until the beans are hard and dry.

The peanut is not really a nut at all; it belongs to the leguminous bean and pea family. Dr. George Washington Carver developed more than 300 by-products from peanuts including food, industrial, and commercial products like dyes, paints, stains, household products, cosmetics, medicines, and beverages.

Snap beans

Pole beans

Peas

Peanuts

L is for the Legume
like lentil, pea, and bean,
deliciously nutritious,
you know what I mean.

Ll

M is for Miniature,
    as tiny as can be—
little plants and flowers
    special 'cause they're wee.

Bonsai (*bone-sigh*) is the art of growing carefully trained, dwarf plants in containers by careful root and stem pruning, coupled with root restriction. The literal translation of the Japanese word bonsai means "to cultivate in a tray." While mostly associated with the Japanese form, "bonsai" originated in China.

Miniature roses are about 24-36 inches in height with buds of about 2-3 inches. Micro-mini roses are the smallest of the miniature rose group. Micro-minis grow 8 to 10 inches tall and flowers range in size from ¼ to ½ inches. Unlike most other modern roses, miniatures are not grafted but grown on their own roots.

Grafting is a method of plant propagation where tissues of one plant are encouraged to fuse with those of another to obtain a desirable characteristic. These characteristics might be cold hardiness, dwarfism, disease resistance, or an aesthetic trait of the plant.

Some hybridized or crossbred plants produce miniature foods including cabbage, lettuce, watermelon, cantaloupe, cucumbers, winter squash, pumpkins, carrots, tomatoes, corn, and eggplants. Wouldn't you like to try some?

M
m

Nut is the general term for a hard-shelled seed, or a hard, dry, single-seeded fruit of some plants. All nuts are seeds, but not all seeds are nuts. The coconut, a basic food in many tropical regions, is misnamed, for this "nut" is not a true nut.

Walnuts, pecans, and chestnuts have the highest antioxidant content of the tree nuts. Walnuts contain omega-3 fatty acids, commonly found in fish, which help to fight heart disease. Almonds contain the same health-promoting monosaturated fats as are found in olive oil. Monosaturated, or healthy fat, can help reduce bad cholesterol levels in your blood and help lower your risk of heart disease. Nuts also contain vitamin E which has antioxidant properties.

Texas is the largest producer of native pecans, and the state tree of Texas is the pecan.

N is for the many Nuts
that people like to eat.
Almonds and walnuts
both make a healthy treat.

Most orchids are epiphytes, the Greek word for air plants, and comprise the largest family of flowering plants in the world.

Vanilla is the only edible fruit of the orchid family. Although there are 150 varieties of vanilla orchid, only two types are used commercially, the *Bourbon* and *Tahitian*. The United States is the largest consumer of vanilla. Today most vanilla used as a flavor and fragrance is synthetic, or manufactured.

The orchid family is huge, with an estimated 25,000 wild species and 1,400 groups, or genera. They grow nearly everywhere in the world including swamps and deserts, in deeply shaded woodlands, and even in the burning sun where lava once flowed. Orchids grow from sea level to 14,000 feet. You can even find them as far north as the Arctic Circle.

Orchid plants range in size from thimble size, like the *Platystele*, to monstrous growths like the *Grammatophyllum,* weighing as much as a bull elephant. Flowers can be the size of a flea up to 8-inch dinner plate size. Orchid seeds are the smallest of all seeds, almost like dust.

Showy Lady's Slipper

Pink Lady's Slipper

Ovenbird

O stands for the Orchid,
that grows most everywhere,
see them in Hawaii
in a hula dancer's hair.

Herbaceous perennial garden plants continue to grow year after year, growing in size and stature until they reach their full maturity. Some common reliable perennials are peonies, iris, phlox, asters, coneflowers, and chrysanthemums. Trees and shrubs are also perennials.

Peonies are one of the oldest plants cultivated, or grown, for their flowers. The Chinese name for the peony is "sho yo" or "most beautiful." Undisturbed clumps of peonies have been reported to be 50, 80, and 100 years old. Peonies attract ants due to the nectar that forms on the outside of the flower buds. The peony is the state flower of Indiana.

The white, strongly scented flowers of jasmine are used as a Hindu symbol for love, while the carnation is a symbol for marriage in China. In Japan the chrysanthemum symbolizes "long life." The sweet iris was named by the Greeks after the goddess of the rainbow.

Several perennial flowers are edible and tasty—including daylilies, hollyhocks, pinks, violets, and yuccas. Never eat a plant or flower unless you know for certain that it is suitable for eating. Many plants are poisonous and could hurt your body.

P p

Bearded Iris

P is for Perennials,
long lasting, strong, and true.
Plant them, and they'll return
year after year for you.

Hosta

Day Lily

Coneflower
(Echinacea)

Shasta Daisy
(Mum)

Pandas, which live in three provinces in southwestern China, feed almost entirely on bamboo leaves, roughly 22 to 40 pounds a day. Most depend on 10 different kinds of bamboo, but they can eat more than 40 different species. The panda has the digestive system of a carnivore, or meat eater, so they cannot properly digest the cellulose, the main substance in the woody part of plants and trees. Pandas spend 11 to 14 hours a day foraging in the wild to keep their digestive tracts full.

Bamboo, a member of the grass family, can grow 1 to 4 feet a day and reach a hundred feet tall.

The letter **Q** also stands for the quaking aspen tree. Aspen trees can send out runners, long slender roots to make new trees. Pando (or The Trembling Giant) is a colony of a single male quaking aspen tree found in Utah. At 80,000 years old, the one massive underground root system is estimated to be among the oldest living organisms in existence.

Q is for Quick growing
plants like the bamboo,
raised to feed the pandas
you might see at the zoo.

The Greeks described the rose as the "Queen of Flowers." It was the flower of the Greek goddess Aphrodite, goddess of love and beauty. The rose was designated as the National Floral emblem of the United States of America on November 20, 1986 by President Ronald Reagan.

Fossil roses, discovered in rock formations in Colorado and Oregon, prove that wild roses date back 40 million years. Strawberries, raspberries, and the hawthorn, as well as apples, peaches, almonds, and apricots are in the rose family, Rosaceae (*rose-Ay-see-ee*).

Rose hips are the fruit of the rose plant and are high in vitamin C. They are used to make jam, jelly, marmalade, and herbal tea. Rose hip soup, *nyponsoppa,* is popular in Sweden. Rose hips have been an important food for native tribes. When supplies of vitamin C-rich citrus fruits were cut off during World War II, rose hips were made into syrup to supply vitamin C to children.

R stands for the Royal Rose,
queen of garden flowers—
symbol for so many things,
beauty, love, and power.

S is for Succulents and cacti,
which grow in regions dry.
They use very little water,
so please give them a try.

Cardon
Cactus

Saguaro
Cactus

Elf
Owl

Gila
Wood-
pecker

Coyote

Barrel
Cactus

Harris Hawk

Joshua Tree

Yucca Glauca

Soaptree Yucca

Beavertail

Southwestern Paintbrush

Agave

Desert Kangaroo Rat

rey's Yucca

Succulent means juicy or fleshy. Succulents are plants having tuberous roots, trunks, or leaves for water storage. Cacti are succulents that usually have spines, which discourages animals from eating them. Some have silver-colored spines that help reflect sunlight to help keep the cactus cool. Cacti have spine cushions called *areoles*, that can produce spines or flowers, but the plants do not have branches or leaves. Succulents do not have *areoles* and can have branches or leaves. There are exceptions like the Christmas cactus, which is a true cactus but does not have spines. There are about 10,000 different types of succulents, and about 2,000 of them are in the cactus family.

The saguaro cactus flower, the state flower of Arizona, grows on the largest cactus found in the United States, the saguaro. Growing only about an inch a year, it can reach a height of almost 40 feet and weigh up to a ton. The saguaro cactus has pleats or folds that allow it to expand to hold a lot of rainwater. It can store enough water to last almost two years.

Ss

T t

A tuber is a thick, fleshy underground stem that stores food and can produce new plants.

A well-known tuber, the potato, is considered the most important vegetable in the world. The Irish Potato Famine was a result of the potato crop failure of 1845. The Irish peasants were almost totally dependent on the potato as a source of food and income, because potatoes produced more food per acre than wheat. The peasants needed the largest crop possible, so they planted a type of potato called "Aran Banner." Unfortunately it was susceptible to a fungus, commonly known as late blight, which destroyed the Irish potato crop.

The All Blue potato is a blue-skinned potato with deep blue, almost purple flesh. Blue potato chips are made from naturally blue potatoes and have a slightly nutty flavor.

A sweet potato is a tuberous root. The darker orange colored sweet potatoes contain more Vitamin A than white potatoes. The cultivation of the sweet potato is being encouraged in Africa where Vitamin A deficiency is a serious problem. Considering complex carbohydrates, fiber content, protein, vitamins A and C, calcium, and iron, the sweet potato ranked highest in nutritional value compared to other vegetables.

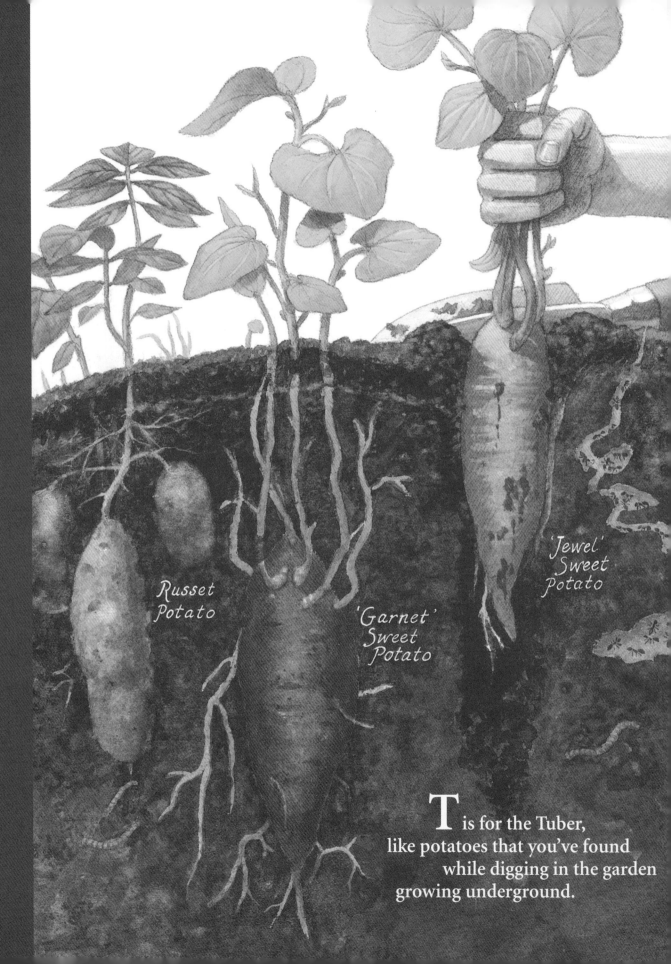

Russet Potato

'Garnet' Sweet Potato

'Jewel' Sweet Potato

T is for the Tuber,
like potatoes that you've found
while digging in the garden
growing underground.

Hybridization is the cross breeding of plants of different varieties in order to produce a new plant with desirable traits from both parent varieties. Thanks to hybridization many fruits and vegetables come in unusual colors like gold raspberries, red and yellow carrots, yellow beets, and even white-skinned pumpkins and cucumbers.

How are these for unusual facts? The mangrove tree of Florida grows on curved roots like stilts in shallow salt water. The banyan tree sends roots down to the ground from its branches, and an old banyan's root system can provide shelter for many people above ground.

The rafflesia is a type of carrion flower, known to have the world's largest bloom, growing 3 feet across and weighing up to 15 pounds. Carrion flowers mimic the smell of rotting flesh and also resemble flesh with their dark red color. Another huge flower, the Titan arum, is also known as the "corpse flower" for its unpleasant odor. Like the rafflesia, the Titan emits the smell of rotting flesh to attract pollinators. Originally from the island of Sumatra, the natives call it "bunga *bangkai*" or "corpse flower."

U is for the Unusual,
plants that you will find
flowers, size, and colors,
of a different kind.

Rafflesia arnoldii

V is for Vegetables
growing in the sun,
eat them fresh or cooked,
enjoy them everyone.

Rhubarb

The fruit or vegetable debate: according to a scientific definition the pumpkin, tomato, capsicum, cucumber, and squash are *fruits* because they all have seeds. However, if you are speaking in cooking or kitchen terms, they can all be properly called *vegetables*.

Vegetables provide many vitamins and minerals. Green vegetables contain vitamin A, dark orange and dark green vegetables typically contain vitamin C, and bushy vegetables like broccoli and related plants contain iron and calcium. Vegetables are low in calories and fats. An ear of corn is about 70 percent water; a potato, 80 percent; and a tomato, 95 percent; while humans are about 75 percent water. Most nutritionists recommend people eat 3 to 5 servings of vegetables or legumes a day. They may be fresh, frozen, canned, or made into juices.

During World War II the United States government urged people to grow Victory Gardens as part of the war effort. Citizens were encouraged to grow their own fruits and vegetables as a way not only to provide food, but to show their patriotism.

V v

Most weeds are nonnative or exotic plants. Many people consider a weed to be any plant that grows where you don't want it to grow. A wildflower normally grows without cultivation in fields, woods, and other unattended places.

Wildflowers are usually considered plants that are native to a region. Many states have chosen an official wildflower. For example, goldenrod is the official state wildflower for South Carolina; Michiganders chose the dwarf lake iris; and Floridians named coreopsis its state wildflower.

Dandelions, considered a pesky weed by many people in the United States, are grown to eat in France. Uncooked dandelion leaves can be eaten raw in salads. They contain 280 percent of an adult's daily requirement of beta carotene as well as half the requirement of vitamin C. They are also rich in vitamin A.

Cattails grow in wet areas. They are an important part of the process of open water bodies being converted to vegetated marshland and eventually dry land. The underground stems of cattails were a major staple for some American Indians, as they were tasty, easy to harvest, and highly nutritious. Some native tribes used cattail "down" to line moccasins and papoose boards, and as tinder to start fires.

Wildflower and Weeds for **W** growing hand in hand, Mother Nature plants them all across the land.

Monarch Butterfly

Wild Coneflower

Pasture Thistle

Oxeye Daisy

X is for Xeriscape,
　a word that you should know;
a way to save on water
　so a garden you can grow.

Aloe Vera

Portulaca

The Denver Water Department coined the term *xeriscape (zir-i-scape)* around 1981 as it sought to help homeowners cope with recurring water shortages in that arid climate. The word is of Greek origin, *xeros*, meaning dry.

Plants adapted to dry or desert conditions are collectively known as xerophytes. Succulents are xerophytes that have developed storage structures in which they hoard water, enabling them to survive periods of drought.

Organic mulch is a layer of material placed on the soil surface to conserve moisture, hold down weeds, and maintain a more constant soil temperature.

Y is for *Your* garden,
whatever it may be,
water garden, windowsill,
rooftop, rock, or topiary.

Topiary is the art of shaping plants by carefully pruning or shearing them into various forms. Topiary was practiced in ancient Rome. Today, England has more examples of this art form than anywhere in the world.

Organic gardeners do not return any inorganic materials like ammonium sulfate, lime, or rock phosphate to the soil. Only organic fertilizers like animal manures or compost are used. Mulching is done using only natural materials like peat moss, bark, grass clippings, cocoa shells, straw, and similar material.

Rooftop gardens reduce air pollution, surface temperatures, and rainwater runoff; insulate buildings against winter cold and summer heat; provide wildlife habitat; and extend the life of the roof. Currently in Chicago, green roofs, or rooftop gardens, cover 2.5 million square feet of downtown roof space.

Hydroculture or hydroponics (growing plants in water) is an easy way to have a windowsill garden. Plants like English ivy, arrowhead plant, and various philodendrons grow well in water.

In 1904 Jennie Butchart began her garden by beautifying a worked-out quarry. Now known as the Butchart Gardens of Victoria, British Columbia designated it as a National Historic Site of Canada in 2004.

Yy

Zz

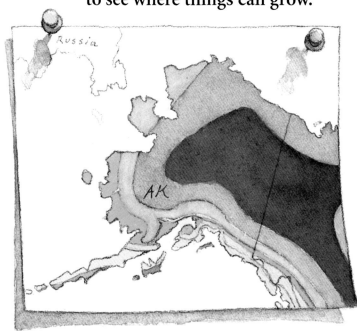

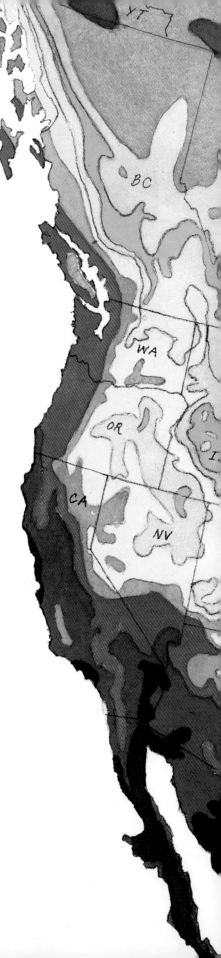

Z is for the many Zones
a special map can show.
Always check for hardiness
to see where things can grow.

Zone maps help gardeners know what plants grow best where they live and when is best to plant them. The United States Department of Agriculture Plant Hardiness Map zones are based on a formula that takes into consideration the average minimum winter temperatures and several other factors affecting plant hardiness including maximum temperature, summer rainfall, snow cover, and wind.

The zones range from Zone 1, where the minimum temperature goes down to minus 50 degrees Fahrenheit, as in Fairbanks, Alaska, to Zone 11, where the minimum low temperatures don't drop below 40 degrees Fahrenheit, as in Honolulu, Hawaii. The data for this map is based on information gathered over a period of 60 years.

The alpine zone is defined as the high-elevation vegetative regions above tree line. Like the arctic tundra, it is characterized by the absence of trees, the short stature of plants, and a low annual mean temperature.

Most planting directions are based on the last frost date for an area, which is the last day in the spring that you might have a killing frost.

NT

NU

NL

B

SK

MB

ON

QC

NL

PE

NB

NS

ND

ME

MT

SD

MN

VT

NH

WI

MI

NY

MA
CT RI

WY

NE

IA

IL

IN

OH

PA

NJ

CO

MO

MD

DE

KS

KY

WV

VA

NM

OK

AR

TN

NC

SC

TX

MS

AL

GA

LA

FL

Mexico

Zone 1 Below −50°F (Below −46°C)

Zone 2 −50° to −40°F (−46 to −41°C)

Zone 3 −40° to −30°F (−41 to −35°C)

Zone 4 −30° to −20°F (−35 −30°C)

Zone 5 −20° to −10°F (−30 to −24°C)

Zone 6 −10° to 0°F (−24 to −18°C)

Zone 7 0° to 10°F (−18 to −13°C)

Zone 8 10° to 20°F (−13 to −7°C)

Zone 9 20° to 30°F (−7 to −1°C)

Zone 10 30° to 40°F (−1 to −4°C)

Zone 11 Above 40°F (Above 4°C)

Eugene M. Gagliano

A passionate gardener since childhood, author Eugene M. Gagliano knows firsthand that children are fascinated with the plant kingdom. Gene is a retired elementary school teacher and the former owner of Mr. Gene's Greens, his own greenhouse. He has had the pleasure of leading his school's garden club for almost 30 years.

Gene is known by many children as the teacher who dances on his desk and continues to inspire others through entertaining and informative author presentations. He was the recipient of the International Reading Association's 2004 Wyoming State Literacy Award and the 2001 Arch Coal Teacher Achievement Award. Gene's other titles with Sleeping Bear Press include two about his home state of Wyoming: *C is for Cowboy: A Wyoming Alphabet* and *Four Wheels West: A Wyoming Number Book*, and his collection of children's poems, *My Teacher Dances on the Desk*.

Gene and his wife, Carol, live at the base of the Big Horn Mountains in Buffalo, Wyoming. He and Carol have enjoyed singing with the Polyester Blends, a professional musical group for 17 years.

Elizabeth Traynor

Elizabeth Traynor has loved both art and nature since childhood, so illustrating this book was a particular pleasure. Working in either scratchboard or watercolor, her illustrations have appeared nationwide for both editorial and advertising clients. She lives in Natick, Massachusetts with her cat, Junebug, and Sammie, a small dog who thinks he is big and loves brussel sprouts. This is the second book she has illustrated for Sleeping Bear Press. She also illustrated *F is for First State: A Delaware Alphabet*